# make**it**yourself

## PAPER & CARDBOARD
## PROJECTS FOR KIDS

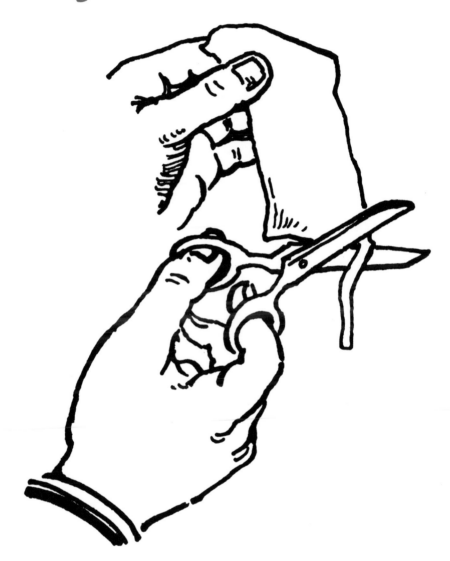

GREEN TIGER PRESS
MMVII

ISBN13  978-1-59583-188-0    ISBN  1-59583-188-6

LAUGHING ELEPHANT BOOKS
3645 INTERLAKE AVENUE NORTH   SEATTLE, WA 98103

WWW.LAUGHINGELEPHANT.COM

# INTRODUCTION • TIPS • SUPPLY LIST

## INTRODUCTION

Creative acts offer such deep joy that we wonder why more people don't seek out opportunities to make things.  This book was created to encourage creativity in young children.

*Make it Yourself: Projects for Kids* is drawn from our huge library of old children's books, periodicals and ephemera. The plethora of craft projects in our holdings was not surprising, given the fewer distractions children had in the late-19th and early-20th centuries.

Despite being tempted by many beautiful but overly complex projects, we have chosen crafts that are appropriate for children seven and up.

Many of the projects suggest pulling out the pages from the book. Those who do not wish to do so can recreate the pages by making color copies, tracing, or simply drawing freehand.

## GLUING ON POSTERBOARD/LIGHT CARDBOARD

Many of these projects need to have parts glued to cardboard. It is easier to glue the whole page or at least the entire area containing the parts of your craft before cutting into the pieces.

After applying  glue or paste and placing the pictures on the cardboard, allow to dry thoroughly, the best way is to put under a weight, such as a pile of books.

If you are having trouble gluing some parts, try double-sided tape (e.g. The window in the street scene, The Sea Serpent to his base, the film holder on Fun Time Movies).

## SUPPLY LIST

To make all of these crafts you will need these supplies:

| | |
|---|---|
| LIGHTWEIGHT CARDBOARD/POSTERBOARD | PAINT |
| GLUE STICK, CLEAR GLUE TUBE OR PASTE | HEAVY SEWING THREAD & NEEDLE |
| PAPERCLIPS | CONSTRUCTION PAPER |
| SCISSORS | MASKING TAPE |
| STRAIGHT SEWING PINS | DOUBLE SIDED TAPE |
| BUTTONS | WAX CRAYONS |
| PENCILS AND PENS | BLUE, RED & GREEN YARN |

# PINWHEEL FUN

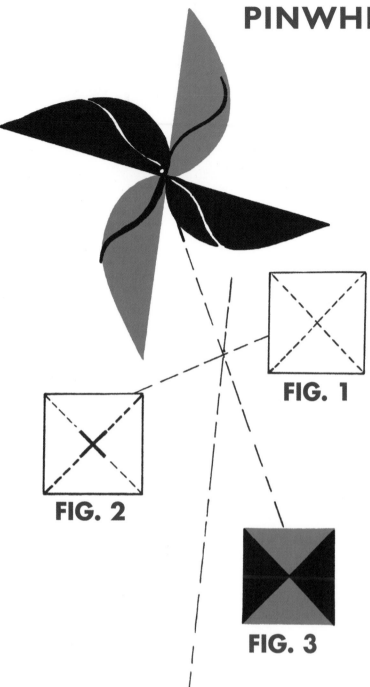

1. To make a pinwheel, cut a piece of paper 4 inches square.
2. Number the corners **1**, **2**, **3**, and **4**.
3. Draw the dotted lines between corners **1** and **3** and corners **2** and **4** (See **FIG. 1**).
4. Then draw an **X** as shown in **FIG. 2**.
5. Color each section, repeat the colors on the opposite side of the paper (See **FIG. 3**).
6. Now cut along the dotted lines up to the **X** at the center of the paper.
7. Then take corner **1** and lay it over the center.
8. Place corner **2** on top of corner **1**. Then put corner **3** on top of corner **2**, and corner **4** on top of corner **3**.
9. Push a pin through all the corners in the center and through a stick or dowel.

Hold your pinwheel against the wind. It will spin.

**FIG. 1**

**FIG. 2**

**FIG. 3**

**FINISHED MODEL**

# PAPER SNOWFLAKES

Paper snowflakes make beautiful ornaments on a Christmas tree. They may be made of light yellow, silver, gold, or white paper. Three thicknesses of tissue paper make perfect snowflakes.

## INSTRUCTIONS

1. You need a square piece of paper. Fold it in the center, then again in halves.
   This will divide the paper into fourths. (See **FIG. 1**)
2. Fold the quarter in half. (See **FIG. 2**)
3. Then draw the outline of a snowflake. (See **FIG. 3**)
4. Cut out the shape, do not cut any folds.
5. Open.

Instead of sketching an outline you may cut free hand the outline of a star. Make narrow slashes all around the outside to give the star a light, airy look. String the snowflakes on a very fine thread. Hang on the branches of the tree.

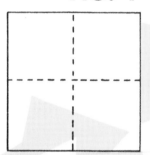

**FIG. 1**

**FIG. 2**

**FIG. 3**

# BUTTON PICTURES

### INSTRUCTIONS

Button pictures are made by gluing, tying, or sewing buttons onto a piece of heavy paper and adding a few ink lines and bits of colored paper to complete the pictures.

Study the sketches given here. Notice how the big buttons are used to make the bodies of the man, the bird, and the cat, and smaller ones for the head, and still smaller ones to make the man's neck, arms, and legs.

You may use colored buttons, such as blue ones for the bird, and black ones for the cat. It's very easy to decorate with pen and ink, and just as easy to fashion the cat's ears and tail and to ink in the cat's whiskers.

You may use these button figures to decorate Valentine, Halloween, and birthday cards.

# JUMPING JACK-IN-THE-BOX

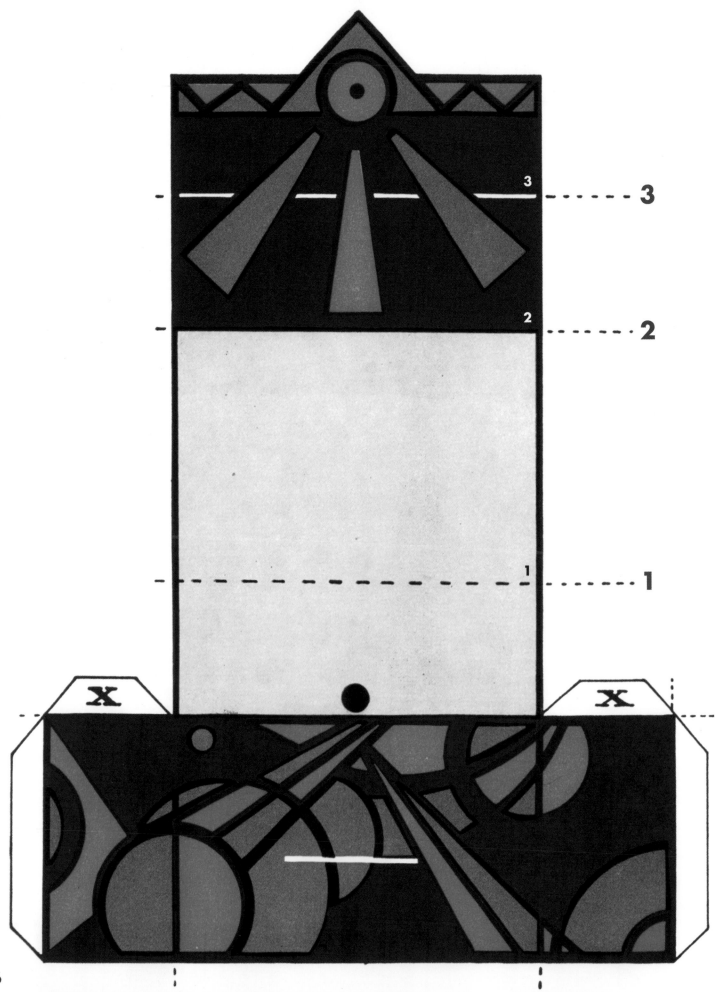

3 - · - · - · - **3**

2 - - - - - · - **2**

1 - · - - - · - · - · - **1**

X                    X

**FINISHED MODEL**

## INSTRUCTIONS – BOX

**1.** Pull out two jumping jack pages and glue on posterboard. Let dry under weight.

**2.** Cut out all pictures on both pages.

**3.** Make a cut on the white line of what will be your box.

**4.** Now bend back along the black line the portion with the black dot above it. Follow this by bending down along the dotted lines **1, 2 & 3**.

**5.** Next bend the tabs marked **X** on the side pieces, and the side pieces themselves, backwards. You will find you have the loose formation of Jack's box.

**6.** Glue the two sides to the bottom by the tabs marked **X** to keep in position.

## INSTRUCTIONS – JACK

**1.** Cut out the design marked **B**.

**2.** Now bend the paper backwards and forwards, concertina fashion, along the dotted lines.

**3.** Next cut out Jack's face and arms, marked **A**.

**4.** Bend back the black and green tab at the bottom and stick it on to the corresponding tab at the top of your folded paper, **B**.

**5.** Now return to the box. Paint the inside of it black.

**6.** Then bend back the black tab at the bottom of the paper **B**, otherwise Jack's body.

**7.** Place it in position and stick it to the center of the bottom of the box.

**8.** Having done this, stick the remaining two tabs to the back of the box, press Jack down firmly on his folds, close the lid, and secure it by slipping the V shape through the cut.

Jumping Jack is now bursting to live up to his name,
a fact you can prove for yourself any time you care to release the lid.

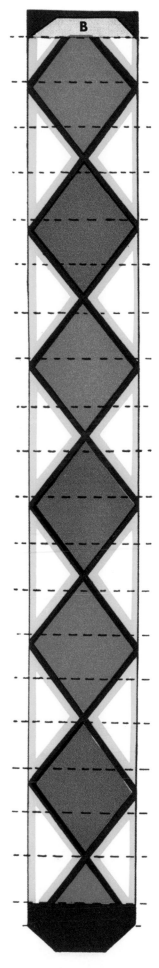

# A PICTURE PUZZLE

1. Pull out this page and glue onto posterboard. Let dry under weight.
2. Cut out all pictures and see if you can solve the puzzle!

# MAY BASKETS

## MATERIALS NEEDED

ROUND CARTONS OR CANS
(OF VARIOUS SIZES)
COLORED
CONSTRUCTION PAPER
CREPE PAPER
PASTE
SCISSORS

**FINISHED MODELS**

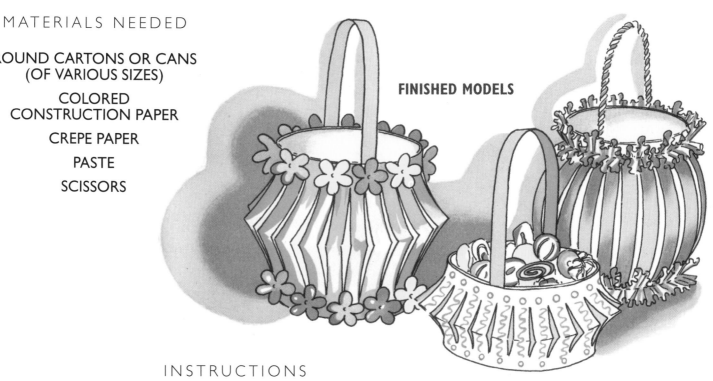

## INSTRUCTIONS

**1.** Cut the strip of paper 1 inch wide for the handle
(tape or staple to sides of carton).

**2.** Now cut piece of paper ½ inch wider than the circumference of the carton
and 3 inches higher than the height of the carton.

**3.** Mark ½ inch margin along the top and bottom of paper.

**4.** Draw a line through the center of the paper.

**5.** Mark and divide the paper into ½ inch strips. Fold paper on center line and
cut vertical lines to the margin.

**6.** Tape or staple margins of paper to carton at top
and at overlap.

**7.** Decorate with crepe paper ruffles and cut-out flowers.

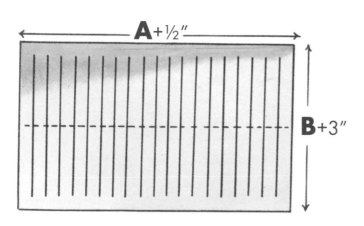

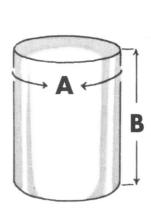

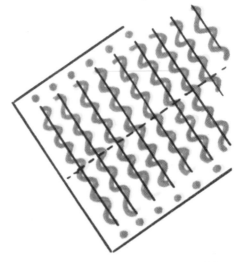

# MUSICAL GLASSES

## INSTRUCTIONS

**1.** Fill a glass with water. Tap it lightly with a spoon. You will discover it gives forth a musical sound. Then pour out some of the water. Note the difference in the musical sound.

**2.** Now arrange 8 glasses in a row on a table. Fill each with water at different levels and sound again. Notice how the pitch can be changed by adding to or reducing the amount of water in the glass. With a little experimenting you can line up the 8 glasses of water and play a scale on them. The key of G is a very good key to which the glasses may be tuned.

**3.** The tapper, a silver spoon, or a slender stick with a wooden ball at the end, and the kind of table upon which the glasses rest, will make a decided difference in obtaining the tones you desire from the glasses.

**4.** After you have the scale adjusted on the glasses, number them **1, 2, 3, 4, 5, 6, 7** and **8**. This will make your playing a tune on them easier. Yes, you can play tunes on these glasses. Try it!

# PECKING ROOSTER TOY

The two roosters on this page and the four strips near the roosters can be put together to make a moveable toy.

### INSTRUCTIONS

**1.** Pull out this page and glue onto posterboard. Let dry under weight.

**2.** Cut out all pictures and parts.

**3.** Now make holes in the strips with a pin, at the black dots.

**4.** Next, glue each rooster to the end of one of the small strips, as shown in the picture of Hilde and Hermann.

**5.** And finally, put the parts of the toy together, pins bent over in the back at the places where the holes are punched.

When the long strips in the finished toy are pushed back and forth, the roosters take turns leaning over as if they are pecking at something on the ground.

# SLIM, SLI & JOHNNY GIRAFFE

## INSTRUCTIONS

1. Pull out this page and glue onto posterboard. Put under weight to dry.
2. Cut out along heavy black lines. Cut out slot with **X** on each end.
3. Carefully match letters and pinholes and fasten together with pins bent over from the back.
4. Insert point of lever in slot (with **X** on each end) before attaching to haystack as shown in small diagram.
5. Move lever from left to right.

# FRANKIE THE FLAG LIEUTENANT

## INSTRUCTIONS

**1.** Pull out this page and glue onto posterboard. Let dry under weight.

**2.** Cut Frankie and his flags out around the black outlines.

**3.** Now get some blue colored yarn, cut a length of it, and make a small loop at one end. Put the other end through this and place it over the blue mark at the bottom of his right arm.

**4.** Wind it firmly around until it meets the blue line at the top.

**5.** Make a small nick in the cardboard to keep the yarn in position, and tuck the end in at the back. This will make one sleeve of his coat.

**6.** Repeat the process on his left arm to form the other one.

**7.** Next, make the lieutenant's trousers, or "slacks" as sailors call them, by taking two longer lengths of yarn, winding them round each leg, starting in both cases by the blue line at the top, and finishing over the blue line at the bottom. Secure the ends as before.

**8.** Next cut out sections **A** and **B,** his flags. Wind red and green yarn around them over the spaces between the lines. Secure the flags to his arms, by sticking his hands over the two black tabs marked **XX.**

**9.** Finally, cut out his ship and glue it over his leg as shown in the illustration; it will then be close at hand, or rather foot, when he is ready to sail!

**FINISHED MODEL**

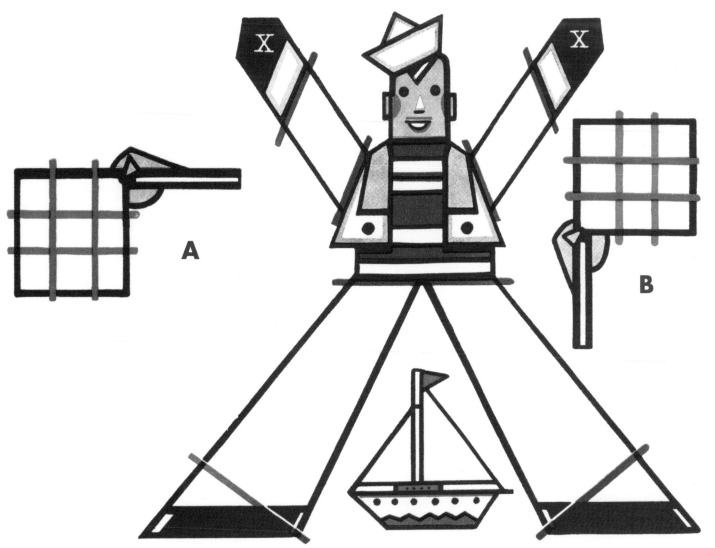

A

B

# DON BLUSTER THE BOLD BAD BANDIT!

### INSTRUCTIONS

**1.** Pull out this page and glue onto posterboard. Let dry under weight. **2.** Cut out around the black outlines.

**3.** Wind colored yarn between the corresponding colored lines in exactly the same way as you do when dressing Frankie the Flag Lieutenant.

**4.** When you come to the green part of his trousers carry the ends of the green yarn upwards and wind it around the blue yarn underneath, at the angle shown in the illustration. This of course applies to both legs.

**5.** When Bluster is properly dressed, color and cut his fearsome weapons.

**6.** Put his sword in his right hand by sticking the yellow part over the black space marked X, and finally, arrange his dagger and pistol snugly in his belt by pushing them down behind the red yarn.

**7.** Now stand him up or hang him on the wall.

**FINISHED MODEL**

make it yourself make it yourself

make it yourself make it yourself

make it yourself make it yourself

make it yourself make it yourself

# CIZZORETTES

Would you believe, from looking at the large drawing below, that all of the small pictures shown here were actually made from parts of a drawing like this?

## INSTRUCTIONS

**1.** Pull out this page and glue onto posterboard. Let dry under weight. **2.** Cut out all shapes.

**3.** Look at illustrations shown for inspiration, and arrange shapes into all sorts of pictures.

**4.** Get busy and see how many things you can make!!

**BLOWING BUBBLES**

**TUG OF WAR**

**FUNNY DUCK**

**JOLLY JUGGLER**

**PLAYING THE FLUTE**

make it yourself make it yourself

make it yourself make it yourself

make it yourself make it yourself

make it yourself make it yourself

# SAVING SAMUEL • PART I

## INSTRUCTIONS

**1.** Pull out this and the following page, and glue them onto posterboard. Let dry under weight.

**2.** Cut out rectangle on this page and all pictures on following page. The rectangle is the playing board for your game.

**3.** Bend back tabs as indicated then glue Samuel to green spot on the playing board and the fish onto red spots.

**4.** You are now ready to play your game.

**FINISHED MODEL**

## RULES FOR THE GAME

Players must stand at least two feet away from playing board. Each player is given the three lifebelts and is allowed three tries to save Samuel by throwing the lifebelts completely over him. Whichever player throws the most lifebelts over Samuel is the winner, the fish don't count for points.

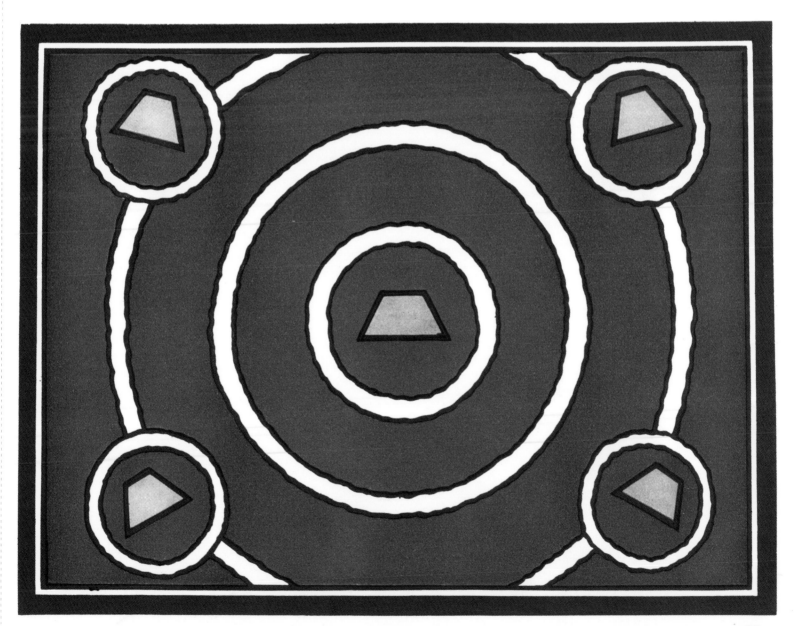

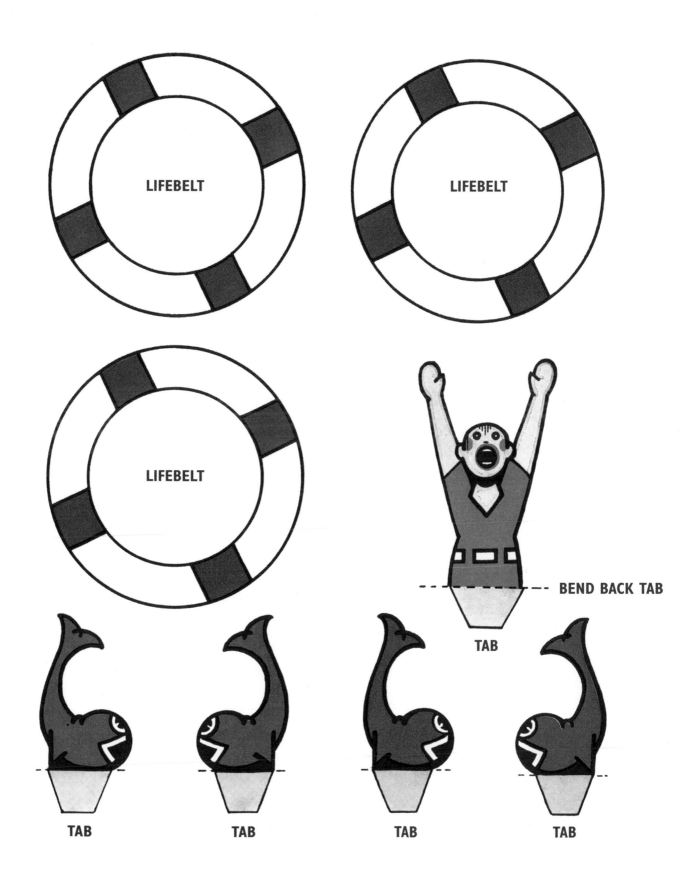

# KIDDYLAND MOVIES • PART I

## INSTRUCTIONS

1. Pull out this and the following page and glue Kiddieland Movies screen and piece marked A/B onto poster-board. Let dry under weight. Do Not glue movie strips to posterboard.

2. Glue or tape A strips on back of screen.

3. Cut movie strips carefully and glue ends as indicated.

4. Insert at right of screen and pull slowly to the left.

5. Use books to hold screen upright, or paste screen in bottom of small box. Cut out section as marked, and turn box on side to imitate a theater.

After using, movie strips may be wound on spools.

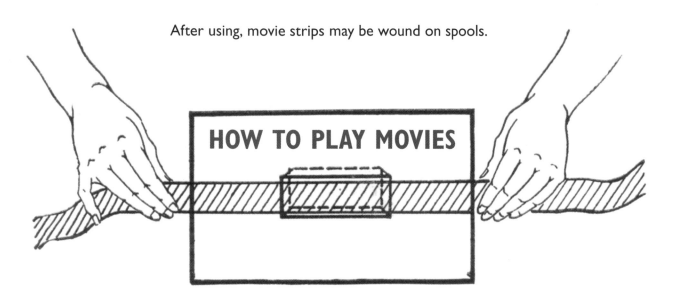

**HOW TO PLAY MOVIES**

Cut out this section

# KIDDYLAND MOVIES • PART 2

A Glue

B

Cut out this piece

Fold forward on the B lines

B

A Glue

# SLIM, SLI & THE BABY ELEPHANT

## INSTRUCTIONS

**FINISHED MODEL**

**1.** Pull out this page and glue onto posterboard. Let dry under weight.

**2.** Cut out along the heavy black lines.

**3.** Carefully match letters and pinholes and fasten with bent pins.

Move back and forth the lever attached to the elephant (See finished model),
and you will see that Slim and Sli are not having an easy time.

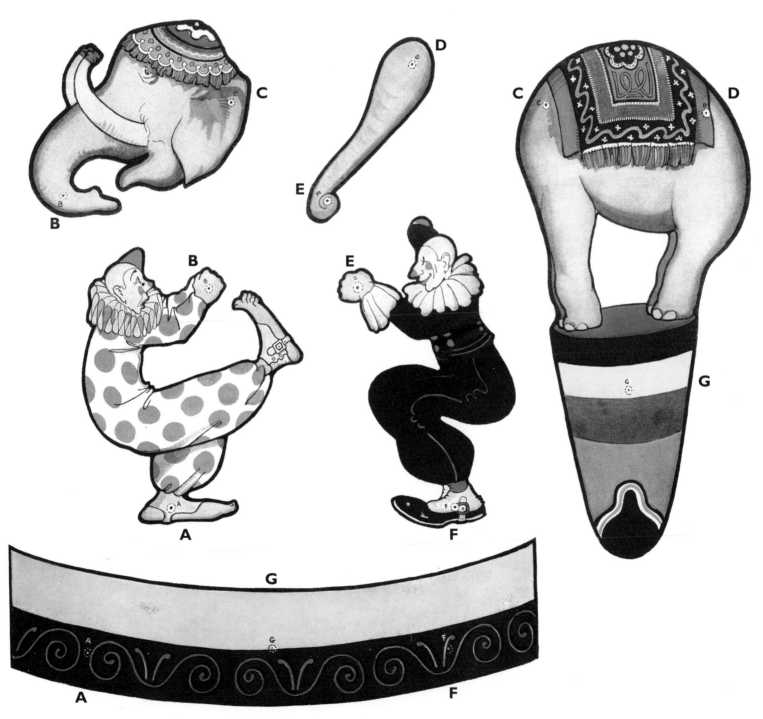

FINISHED MODEL

# SCOTTIE THE PERKY PUPPY

## INSTRUCTIONS

**1.** Pull out this page and glue it onto posterboard. Dry under weight.

**2.** Cut out the two sections of Scottie's kennel, paint the reverse side black, and pierce hole at the bottom of the white ring.

**3.** Next bend back the two sides, also the red tab marked **A**.

**4.** Bend kennel back on lines until red tab marked **A** overlaps. Then glue the two parts together. Now bend inwards the four red tabs at the top.

**5.** After you have bent the roof, **SECTION 2**, downwards along the middle line, place it in position on these and stick down.

**6.** Next cut out Scottie himself, paint him black on the reverse sides and stick him together (all except his ears and the lower part of his body and legs, as shown by the dotted line) and pierce a hole through the white dot on his pretty collar.

**7.** Now bend his ears slightly downward and his legs outwards.

**8.** To make quite sure that he does not run away, cut a piece of string about 6 ½ inches long, and thread it from the collar to the ring on his kennel.

**9.** A few pieces of straw, or paper, will make Scottie a comfortable "bed".

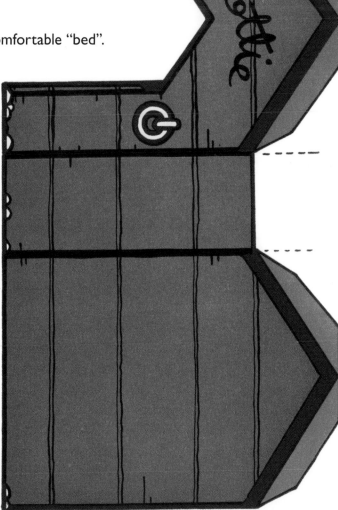

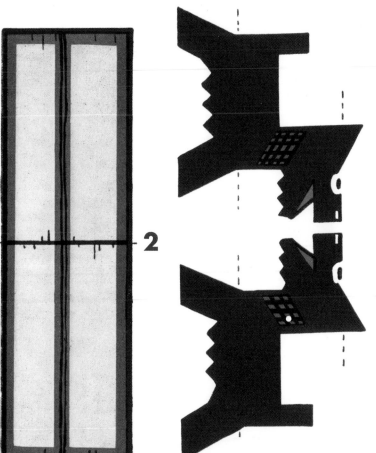

# SEA SERPENT

## INSTRUCTIONS

1. Pull out this page and glue onto posterboard. Let dry under weight.
2. Cut out the three green and white strips in one piece and glue it to a thin piece of cork or Styrofoam.
3. Now cut around the outlines, and pierce four holes where indicated by white dots.
4. Join the three sections together with needle and long piece of thread pushed through the four holes and knotted.
5. You will now have three separate strips, which will form the serpent's base. After having cut out the main **SECTIONS 1, 2** and **3,** comprising the serpent's head and tail, glue short lengths of toothpick behind them, level with the bottom lines, and in turn glue or tape these over the black lines on their respective stands.

Sea Serpent is now complete and will no doubt wag his tail in anticipation of exciting voyages to come!

# DANGLING DAN

## INSTRUCTIONS

**1.** Pull out this page, Do Not glue Dan onto posterboard. **2.** Cut out on all heavy black lines.

**3.** Fasten the arms to the tabs formed by bending the triangles near head forward on dotted line.

**4.** Bend tabs on back of head forward, glue face and cap to these.

**5.** Bring the waist together in front and fasten by pasting big black button over front line.

**6.** Make each leg round by bringing opposite sides together and fastening tab to opposite side so as to hold in place.

**7.** Bend foot outward to make him stand on feet. Crease legs slightly where they are attached to body

**8.** Cut out collar and place around Dan's neck were cut is.

**9.** With a needle and thread, pierce a hole in Dan's cap and make a long loop of thread, tying off with knot at end.

Jerk the thread, and he flings his legs about in comical gestures.

# A SPINNING TOP

INSTRUCTIONS

**1.** Pull out this page and glue onto posterboard. Let dry under weight..

**2.** Cut out both pieces of the top.

**3.** Pierce a hole through the small white circle on **SECTION I**.

**4.** Bend **SECTION 2** backwards to form a cone.

**5.** Secure both ends by sticking the blue tab over the green. Turn the green and blue painted tabs inward and stick directly in the middle of the reverse side of **SECTION I**.

**6.** Push a sharpened pencil through both holes, put a blob of glue top and bottom to prevent slipping.

Turn the pencil sharply between finger and thumb, and, hey presto! You have a spinning top.

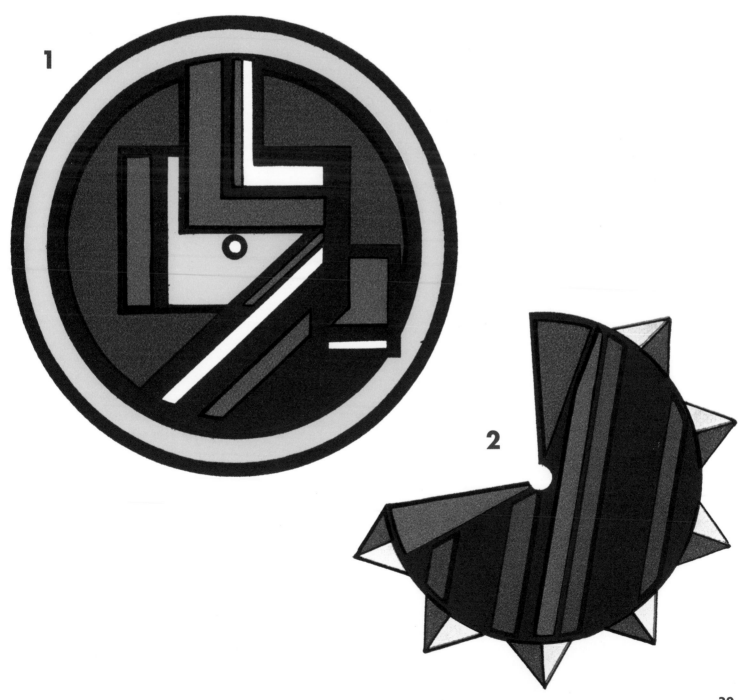

# SWING-HIGH SWING-LOW! • PART I

INSTRUCTIONS

**1.** Pull out this and the following page and glue onto posterboard. Let dry under weight.

**2.** Cut out 3 parts along heavy black lines.

**3.** Pierce two holes at the extreme top of the moon, where the two red dots are; also through the two black dots in the little squares of Pierrette's hands as well as the other dots on the blue parts, the seat of the swing, as indicated by the red dotted lines.

**4.** Next take two pieces of red thread, or fine string, each about 5 inches long, knot them at one end and thread the other ends from the front through the holes in the seat of the swing, then through the back of the holes in Pierrette's hands, and yet again through the front of the two holes at the top of the moon.

**5.** Pull the string through these last holes until Pierrette's toes clear the highest cloud by about ½ inch.

**6.** When you have made sure that both sides of the string are level with the seat, knot them at the back, cutting off the ends.

**7.** Now turn the design face downwards and stick a small weight of any kind- a button will do- at the back of the figure, directly in the middle of the lower part of the little lady's back.

**8.** Now bend back the two red tabs at the bottom of the clouds and stick them in their places on the stand below.

**9.** Lastly, to make the whole model stand firmly upright, glue a match-box over the yellow space marked **M**, in turn gluing it to the back of the clouds.

**FINISHED MODEL**

By blowing on the front of the figure, you can make Pierrette "swing high" in a most natural way, winning the steady approval of you and the man in the moon.

2

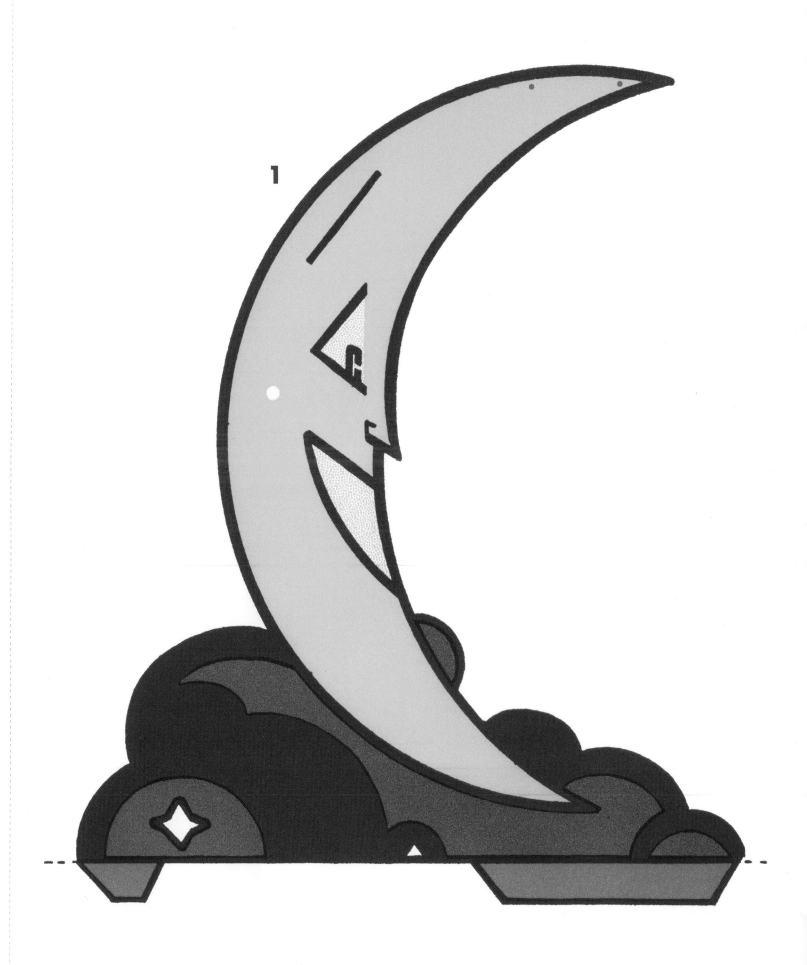

# THE CHIC CHICKEN

### INSTRUCTIONS

**1.** Pull out this page and glue onto posterboard. Let dry under weight.

**2.** Read instructions by pictures for what to do, and then cut out when ready to put the Chic Chicken together.

**3.** Make sure to fold on dotted lines and tabs, and cut the two black lines on the chicken's body for his wings.

Here's half his hat.

Here's the other half.

Here's his little tie to make him look nice and neat and well dressed.

Here's half of the little chicken.

Here are his little wings to help him jump the puddles.

Here's his other half.

Here's his little cane, so he can strike a pose or lean on it when he's tired.

Here's his little suitcase, so he can pretend he has alot more clothes than you can see here.

Here's one of his spats to keep his little left leg warm.

Here's his other spat, so he won't look lopsided.

make it yourself make it yourself

make it yourself make it yourself

make it yourself make it yourself

make it yourself make it yourself

# RACING TURTLES

### INSTRUCTIONS

**1.** Pull out this page and glue onto posterboard. Dry under weight.

**2.** Cut out turtles.

**3.** Color them very well on both sides with wax crayons, to make them waterproof, so they can float.

**4.** Bend legs down, feet up, and head up.

**5.** Place turtles in water. Blow gently from behind and watch them race!

# LAURENCE THE LEOPARD

## INSTRUCTIONS

**1.** Pull out this page and glue onto posterboard. Let dry under weight.

**2.** Bend his neck downward along the dotted line **B**, and upward along **A**.

**3.** Bend his legs forward along dotted line **C** and backward along **D** and **E**.

**4.** Bend his tail forward and the green tabs backward.

Perched in this pleasing position, he will look great when completed if he is glued, tabs and tail, to a stand of circular cardboard 6 inches in diameter, which has been colored red.

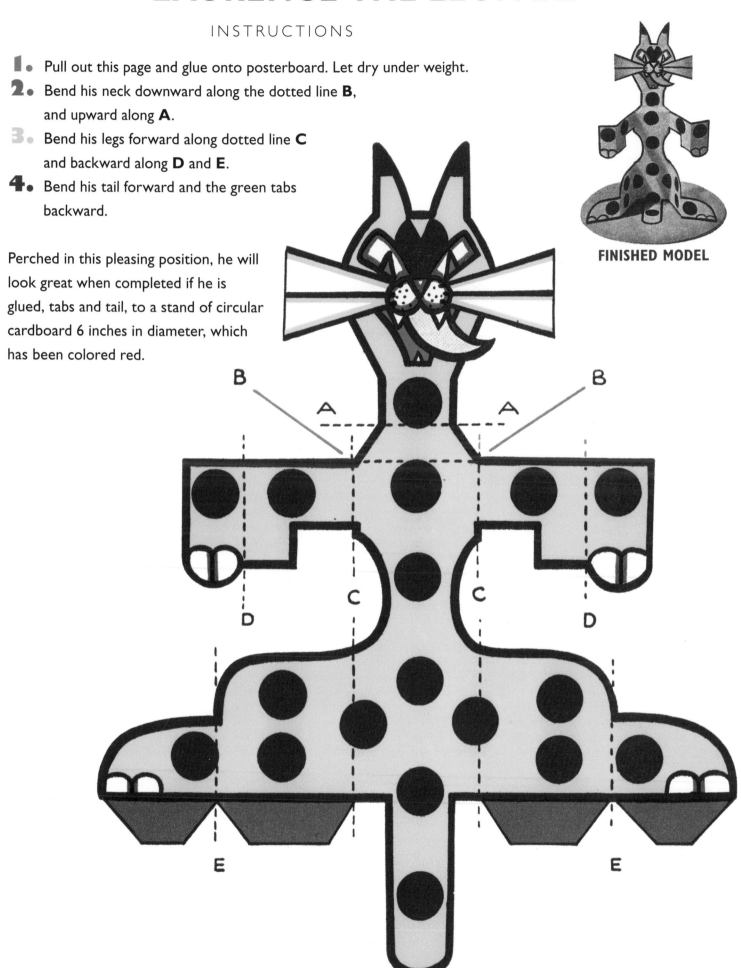

**FINISHED MODEL**

49

# JUMPING JOE • PART I

## INSTRUCTIONS

1. Pull out this page and glue onto posterboard. Let dry under weight
2. Cut all the shapes out.  3. Now color Joe.
4. Make tiny holes as indicated by circles, by pushing pin through.
5. Put pieces together, matching letters with one another, and joining by pins that are bent over in back.
6. Then in the same manner fasten cardboard strips **C** to the ends of the **B** strips.
7. Next fasten cardboard strips **D** and **E** to the end of strips **C**.
8. In the exact center of each **E** strip punch a tiny hole. .
9. Fasten these strips together as shown. Fasten legs to ends of **E** strips, being careful that the feet are turned in opposite directions.
10. Turn Joe over and put tape over pins that have been bent in back.

When assembled, the reverse side of Jumping Joe should look like the second drawing. His hat is red. His hair is yellow. His eyes are blue. His lips are red. His mittens are red. His shoes are black. His stockings are red. His body (**B, C, D** and **E**) is blue. To operate, pull arms out as far as they will go, then push them together as far as possible. You can also put a piece of string or thread in Joe's hat, and dance him around that way. You will be surprised at the funny things you can make Joe do.

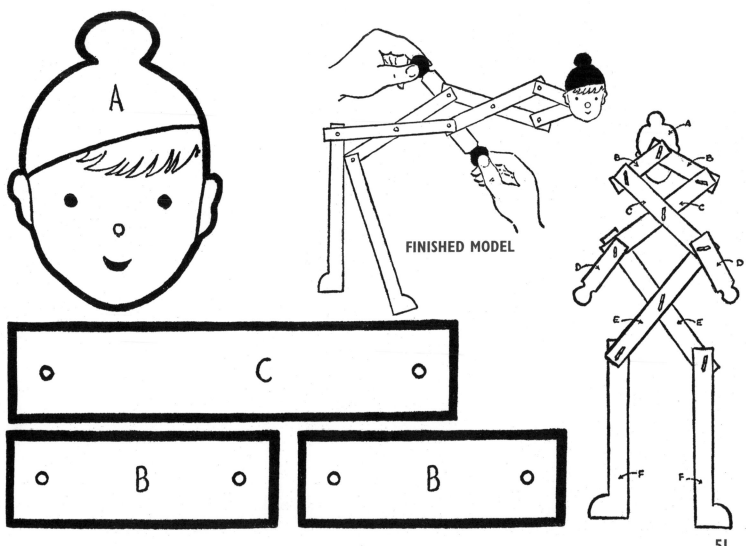

**FINISHED MODEL**

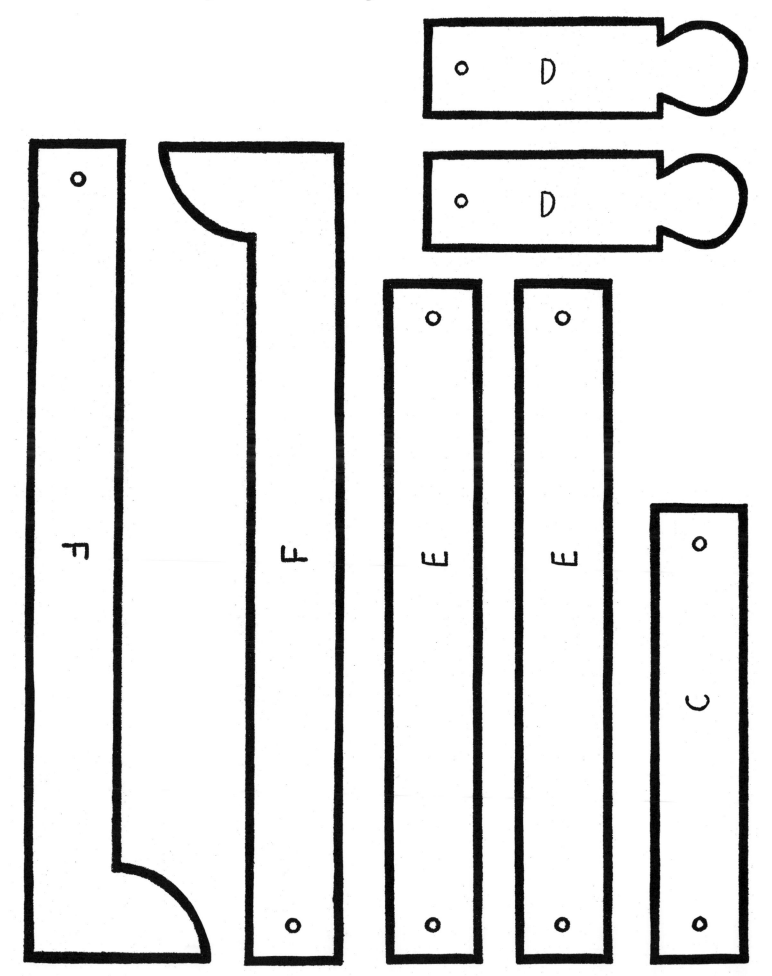

# A SPARKLING PAPER PIPE

**FINISHED MODEL**

INSTRUCTIONS

**1.** Start with a strip of posterboard/lightweight cardboard 3 inches wide and 11 inches long.

**2.** Cut the hole (**A**) in one end (See **FIG. 1**)  **3.** Glue the 2 lengthwise edges together to form a hollow tube.

**4.** Staple closed the end nearest the hole (See **FIG. 2**)

**5.** Cut the bowl of pipe, like the shape in the picture, about 4 inches across the widest part (See **FIG. 3**)

**6.** Cut slashes on the lower edge and paste the pipe-bowl into a funnel shape by bringing the 2 sides together (See **FIG. 4**)

**7.** Fasten the bowl over the hole in the stem, glue in place (See **FIG. 5**)

Make some confetti by tearing or cutting pieces of colored and sparkly paper into small pieces, then fill the bowl of the pipe and blow!

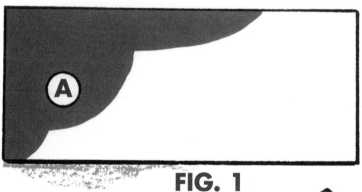

**FIG. 1**

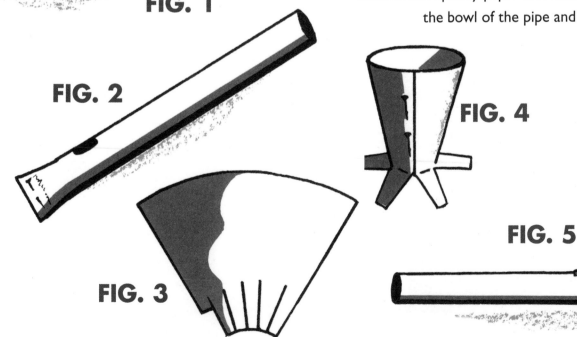

**FIG. 2**

**FIG. 3**

**FIG. 4**

**FIG. 5**

# ROCKING HORSE • PART 1

## INSTRUCTIONS

**1.** Pull out the following page and glue double rocking horse onto posterboard. Let dry under weight.

**2.** Cut out along lines.

**3.** Fold the cut-out double horse in half so that the 2 sides match.

**4.** Fasten the 2 sides of the horse's back together with a paper clip.

**5.** Bend the base up between the rounded ends of the rockers.

Give the small rocking horse a gentle push, it will start rocking back and forth!

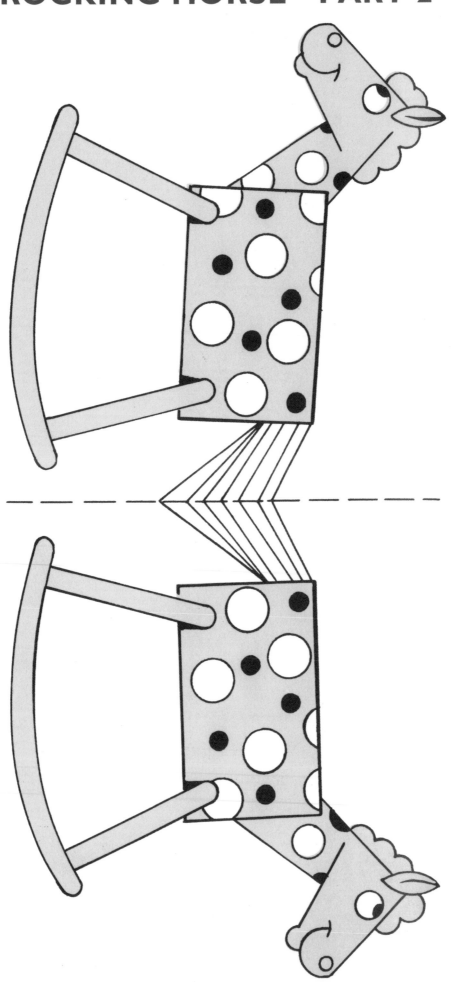

# STREET SCENE

INSTRUCTIONS

**1.** Pull out this page and glue onto posterboard.
Let dry under weight.

**2.** Cut out the two main **SECTIONS** 1 and 2, also cut out the
white space of the shop window, marked **A**.

**3.** Now bend the two yellow parts of **SECTION** 2 forward and
the black tabs backward. If you have it handy, stick a piece of
cellophane evenly over the window parts to represent glass.

**4.** Next bend the lower white part of **SECTION** 1, the roadway, forward along the dotted line and place
**SECTION** 2 in position behind the cut-out window so that the bottom line is level with the bottom line of
the shop front, and stick the two sections together by the black tabs at the sides of **SECTION** 2, (over which
you have previously stuck the cellophane) with glue or double sided tape.

**5.** To complete the scene, cut out the mailbox, bend the green tab backwards, and car, bend the
green tab backwards and stick them in the positions indicated.

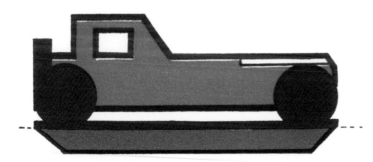

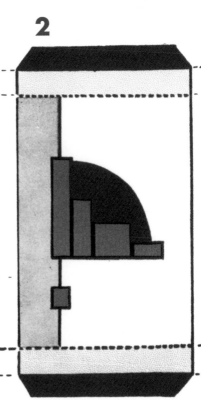

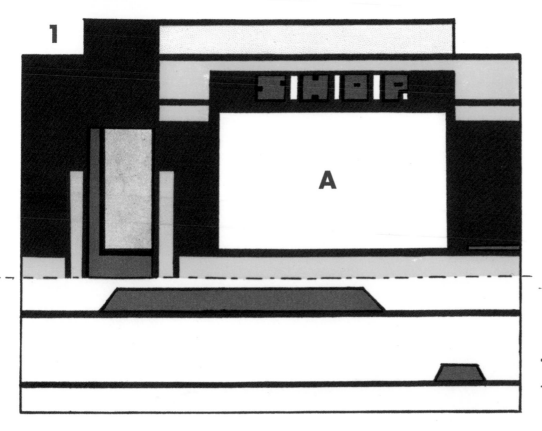

# HATS, CAPS & BANDS

JUGO-SLAVIA · ·
DRUM MAJOR · ·
GREECE ·
NORWAY
PHILIPPINES · CHINA · ·
POSTMAN · ·
GERMANY ·
SPAIN ·
BELLHOP · ·

## HATS CONSTRUCTED WITH OATMEAL-SALT AND HAT BOXES ·

MEDIEVAL ·
BONNET
BONNET
CHINESE NATIVE ·
FINISHED MODEL
MONGOLIA
CLOWN ·

## EXPERIMENT WITH CIRCLES TO MAKE HATS ·

DUTCH ·
SPAIN ·
TURKEY ·
NURSE ·
INDIAN · ·

## MODIFIED RECTANGLES · FOLDED AND PASTED · TO MAKE CAPS AND BANDS

## HATS FOR HALLOW'EEN PARTIES · PLAYS AND PARADES ·

COOK

## PAPER SACK HATS

PAT GREENE

# PICTURE CREDITS

Front cover    Louise D. Tessin. From *Something to Do for Every Day,* 1928.

Endpapers    From *Monerias Geometria-Plana,* n.d.

Frontispiece    Cecily Steed. From *Things to Make,* n.d.

2    From *Things to Make and Do,* 1969.

3    From *Things to Make and Do,* 1969

4    From *Things to Make and Do,* 1969.

6 - 7    From *Modern Playcraft,* c. 1930.

9    Louise D. Tessin. From *I Made it Myself,* n.d.

11    Magazine illustration, 1950.

12    From *Things to Make and Do,* 1969.

13    Magazine illustration, 1952.

15    Berta & Elmer Hader. Magazine illustration, 1924.

17    From *Modern Playcraft,* c. 1930.

19    From *Modern Playcraft,* c. 1930.

21    Magazine illustration, 1937.

23    From *Modern Playcraft,* c. 1930.

25    From *Modern Playcraft,* c. 1930.

27    Thomas Lamb. Magazine illustration 1922.

29    Thomas Lamb. Magazine illustration 1922.

31    Berta & Elmer Hader. Magazine illustration, 1924.

33    From *Modern Playcraft,* c. 1930.

35    From *Modern Playcraft,* c. 1930.

37    Magazine illustration, 1918.

39    From *Modern Playcraft,* c. 1930.

41    From *Modern Playcraft,* c. 1930.

43    From *Modern Playcraft,* c. 1930.

45    Magazine illustration, 1919.

47    R.O.B. Magazine illustration, 1956.

49    From *Modern Playcraft,* c. 1930.

51    Magazine illustration, 1947.

53    Magazine illustration, 1947.

55    From *Things to Make and Do,* 1969

56 - 57    From *Things to Make and Do,* 1969

59    From *Modern Playcraft,* c. 1930.

61    Pat Greene. Magazine illustration, 1939.

Back Cover    Kayren Draper. From *Round About You,* 1935.